A TRAVELLING

Soul

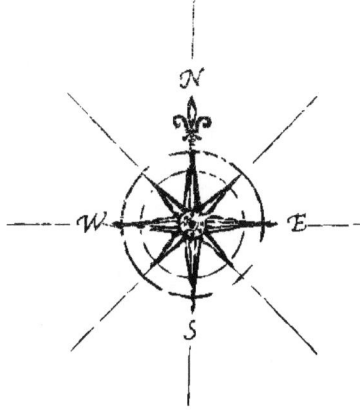

a poetic journey

by

Lizzy in words

Printed in the United States of America

First Printing, 2020

ISBN 978-1-949321-17-3

All writings within this book belong to the author.

Cover Art Image by: lizzy in words

A.B.Baird Publishing
66548 Highway 203
La Grande OR, 97850
USA
www.abbairdpublishing.com

for your love

that's been a constant

with the ebbing of life's sea

across the stars, another world

wherever you may be

your love lives on

inside of me

like any other story

it begins with the same line

of once upon a time

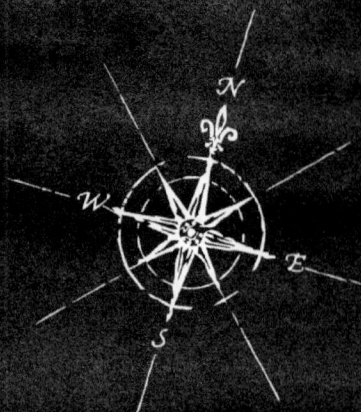

I

TO THE PAST

if I write about us
should I only tell the good
when the bad has also shaped me
should I avoid the things
that made my heart a patchwork
of stitched together pieces
should I not tell it all
of how the golden lines came to be
should I not tell my truth
after all
it makes me, me

no secrets

let us set sail to the beginning
when the sea was calm
and the sky still clear
when a child was still growing
like a little seed
that full of love was planted
inside her mothers' womb
unaware of what was yet to come
but before the waves would crash her
there was still time to enjoy
all the love her mother gave her
from the day that she was born

born

a mother's heart so overjoyed
filled with so much love
for this little life that came to be
yet always fearful of repeating
her own history
love was not always known to her
she came with a bruised heart
could she make different choices
carve out her own path
I can tell you she had nothing
to ask forgiveness for
for I have grown beneath her beating heart
and from the day that I was born
no one could love me more

a mother's love

tears of innocence
a young child cried
this giant world before her eyes
an old soul of a sensitive kind
feeling as though ripped from the stars
a sense of not quite fitting in
already lost yet still to begin
in a world with so much untapped potential
she would treasure the small and simple things
like how the stars laughed and the songbird sings
and the flowers swayed with the changing wind
and she'd wait for other old souls while she grew
who would see all the beauty that she'd come to know
and this world would show her glimpses of home
so this little child would feel less alone

innocent eyes

BREATHE MY CHILD

OPEN YOUR EYES

AND BREATHE

a small ember was set ablaze
when a child was taught about faith
faith in love and the sacrifice
that was made to keep us all alive
faith in more than what the eyes can see
of the father who has faith in me
and with every word she learned
her soul felt closer to its home
for that little child had always known
and was very much aware
that the path of faith
would come with loss and despair
but also the greatest love of all
and wonders big or small
a tether anchoring the soul
reminding it of its goal
of all that it came here to do
before it can come back to you
the source of all creation
growing is what faith must do
without limitation

spark

I wish I could tell you

your life would be easy

that you would always feel loved

and no one would ever break your heart

I wish I could have told you

to treasure every moment when you felt truly happy

and that the good would always outweigh the bad

that you wouldn't feel lost

and never feel sad

I wish I could tell you

that your heart would be too big for this world

and that you give too many chances

even when they are no longer deserved

I wish I could tell you

that those who were supposed to lift you up and protect you

would end up hurting you the most

...

...

I wish I could tell you
that the world wouldn't judge you
and its darkness wouldn't try to dim your light
I wish I could tell you
that you wouldn't have to fight
I wish I could tell you
you'd have to be your own hero
and every word you needed to hear
I wish I could tell you
to never give up on your dreams
and to grow a thick skin
if I could have told you all I know now
do you think it would be different
who we might have been

if I could tell you

even in the beginning
there was something
darkness and He
bringer of light

would we know what light is
if not for some darkness
in shadows
casting contrast in life

yet light is always stronger
as it chases the dark away
and He made it bright and beautiful
on creations very first day

there was light

you've always been an inspiration

a stronghold where I felt safe

the one, who at times

I would try to imitate

as we'd step out into nature

the adventures we would undertake

for knights and dragons

were born from imagination

and many have we slain

ships we've sailed and harbours conquered

pirates, young and wild

no limit to where it could take us

you were my hero then

in a time where all could be

and everything was

but in all honesty

sometimes I wish we could go back

to that land of forgotten fantasy

where kings and queens would rule

the simple days

just you and me

siblings

it took me a long time to see
that even trough suffering
beauty can be born

every word you spoke to hurt me

came from your own pain

I only wish

that I had known that then

for my fragile heart

sensitive and kind

was broken, not once

but many, many times

for I always thought

it was a true reflection

of me, through your eyes

reflection

I've never known how much you loved me
because I never understood
why you pulled away and turned inside yourself
hiding from moments I longed to share
I always thought you didn't care
I never knew what was going on within you
and I was too small to understand
why we couldn't communicate
that this, feeling absence of love, didn't mean hate
that it didn't mean I was unwanted, not enough
but that it was within yourself that it was rough
how no one ever taught you to express
with words, emotion and love
I wish I could have told you then
how you were not alone
so it wouldn't have taken us a lifetime
to get to know each other
to learn how much we are alike
all this pain it would have saved
for both of us and those we may have hurt
who got caught in the middle
of our broken hearts
love was never truly absent
just hidden from the start

absent love

to everyone who's ever told me I'm too quiet

your lack of knowledge and understanding

does not define my voice

I know that now, but way back when

you took my self-confidence

a young child should be supported

to grow at its own pace

and now that I look back at it

my voice, it had no place

between your voices that were so loud

where no one would truly listen

to that little child

I saved my voice for those

who loved me as I am

and when I felt safe

my voice was present

and silence had no place

so do not tell a child that it's too quiet

but humble yourself with understanding and grace

for when you've earned to see

the true colours of that child

you might be amazed

and grateful you were kind

silent voices

WHEN HER VOICE

WAS SILENCED

SHE LEARNED

HOW TO SING

we all love in our own way
sometimes love is hidden
in the small and simple things
love does not equal exuberance
and doesn't always sing
for love can be overwhelming
as it instigates a change
and change is often scary
for love, it makes us more
it's something we often fight
yet if embraced, within it
your own voice will be found
for love, it cannot grow
if it is not by choice
to let it be completely free
and grow into all that it was meant to be

let love grow

you've always thought
the world needed saving
and that somehow that task was yours
but how was a child to solve such issues
how was a child to endure
yet many gathered their pain around you
entrusting you with heavy words
as if their souls knew yours was safe
but it was so far out of place
for no matter what you did before
you were sent upon this earth
you were only just beginning
to awaken and to learn
and yet patiently you listened
though your voice was barely heard
absorbing more than you could carry
but little child
you were never meant to be
the saviour of this world

saviour

troubled waters did I swim
no more time for lingering
to float in peaceful harmony
choices that were made for me
a forest so thick I could no longer see
that somewhere in-between the trees
a field of flowers was awaiting me
flowers in buds, waiting to bloom
with every bud that would unfold
I would come closer to the road
that would lead me to my inner voice
the power of my own choice

Troubled waters

branches breaking by strong winds
as birds flocked together between its leaves
in search of shelter within this tree
but the bark, it weakened as its leaves fell
for so many secrets, the birds came to tell
yet the tree, it kept giving
for its nature was so
wondering if, the birds would ever know
how it wished to uproot
and just walk away
to be free of this burden
if just for one day

The giving Tree

let me sit here by the water
to slowly catch my breath
it isn't easy growing up
and I am not there yet
I am just at the beginning
of what is to unfold
and already, at times
do my bones feel old
but I will come to cherish
every moment that is quiet
every breath that I can take
without feeling the world
and its heavy weight

pause

YOU WERE BORN

BECAUSE HE BELIEVES

YOU ARE WORTHY

OF LIVING

many times have I rebelled
and strayed from His path
and even then He stood by me
like a patient father
waiting for my tantrum to be over

Tantrum

do you not know, that stardust lies
hidden where your soul resides
it's also where your dreams are born
where many will stay untouched, forlorn
maybe that is, why at night
you are gazing at the sky
looking for that single star
to point you towards the place
where the dust and dreams
are secretly made

but all you need to know
is that stardust has always been within you
and that single star will not speak of dreams
as they are untouched reality
there's no need to search
for what is already there
once you awaken, all is laid bare
and once time feels the need
for you and that star to meet
it will ask you
do you now see, that the stardust in you
makes you a child of me?

origins

THE BRIGHTEST STARS

ARE ALWAYS BORN

UNDER THE GREATEST

PRESSURE

we are all born in innocence
I was nothing different
until life became defected
and my body a broken shell
I have looked for answers
wherever they could be found
my journey is far from over
it seems to be of the unending kind
and though I have shed many tears
life taught me many lessons
I'd like to share them with you here
walk with me through life's confessions

Teachings

my mind was the only escape
of the pain tearing my flesh away
as if someone crushed my ribs
and tore out all the bones
slicing all the nerves
pain I hope, you'll never know
moments when my mind
my fantasy
was the only thing
saving me

chronic pain

it took me falling to my knees

begging you to listen to me

to try and understand

not to judge but hold my hand

to open up your eyes

and to truly see

that this was not my choice

that this battle was taking

everything from me

begging

arms of lead

too heavy for feet to tread

with every day

another piece eaten away

everything that's asked

feels like a Herculean task

spoken words cannot be unsaid

all of them in judgement

for understanding do they lack

and it is not the battle with the beast

that is the heavy part

but all the words spoken behind the back

that weigh most heavy upon the heart

survive

she had battled

many wars

the inside

of her body

was riddled

with scars

when the world screams at you
telling you there's nothing wrong
when all you feel is how you're coming undone
then doubt fills your mind
because, what if they're right
what if everything you feel
and everything you've said
was ever only in your head
even though that voice inside
tells you something isn't right
that everything you feel is real
so when you're close to giving up
you finally learn to trust
that only you know how you truly feel

...

...

that all these screams your body gives
should have never been ignored
that sometimes people are too blind
too look beyond the things they know
too caught up in their ego
to admit they are not all knowing
until you find that one person
who makes the pieces fit
who finally acknowledges every word you've ever said
how it has never been inside your head
and you're no longer alone
to carry this burden, all this pain
only you know you
and listening to that voice
will never be in vain

Trust yourself

life can be as brittle
as a freshly frozen lake
you might cross it
without a single break
the ice, though thin, still intact
some may only get halfway
before it gives, then it's too late
and many just begin
to place one single step
as gentle as can be
before it shatters, just like glass

brittle

I would give you the air inside my lungs
if it meant you could keep on breathing
I would give you my life, my beating heart
if it meant yours could go on a little longer
for in my eyes, you deserve the world
and I wish I could lay it at your feet
that I could teach you to survive
the darkness that's to come
but if you must leave, then know
that my breath is breathing you
and my heart, will pull through
for every beat is you and life is nothing
if not entanglement of souls
so I will walk along the shore
as you drift into the water
and when you are no more
I will come back to the water
and drench myself with you
so I can feel you just a little longer

entanglement

43

she lit up the world
like the rising sun
and every time she smiled
a glow of warmth and tenderness
would cast some magic deep inside
of everyone she ever met
and when you were blessed
to feel her embrace
a love so delicate
like a blanket of lace
would wrap itself around you
and the world for one moment stood still
and your breath would find a steady pace
while your heart no longer felt, it had to race
for in that moment you would just be
loved in all your entirety

her glow

He came down from heaven

to carry your light

as we sat beside you

I whispered it would be alright

if you wanted to go

and say goodbye

for as long as I longed to hold you

your body was in pain

and so He sent His angel

to take you home again

gone

if tears could have a colour
mine would be ruby red
from all the pain, a broken heart
and words that went unsaid

yet red of love, they'd also glow
for how much love I've got to know
and whatever time life gave to us
it would never have been enough

ruby red

capture me

in heartbeats

tears and laughter

in memories that make

the bad days softer

capture me in dewdrops

as your feet make their way

through the grass

where the bees awaken

and nature springs

capture me

in the gentle breeze

caressing the bird's wings

capture me

in all the little things

enclosed

and there it was

like lightning splitting a tree

an eruption of sadness

tears flowing free

so much hurt locked up inside

ever since that day

eyes now overflowing

tears finding a way

pushed down in the abyss
of a lost soul and muttering sorrow
are the tears that should be cried
hurt that should come out

slumber

flowers would grow
where her feet had tread
while into the forest she was lead
by a song that came upon the wind
a history that drew her in
and further down between the trees
nature engulfed her in beauty

for in that moment she could be
there was no loss of memory
no frozen time or rivers cried
and all she was and all she is
would simply just exist

eternal

it's all in there
in the trenches of my soul
like freckles spread out across my skin
every breath filled with sadness
every tear that captured happiness
all the scars that make me who I am
they are all loved and sometimes hated
as they run deep into the darkness
where light fights hard to stay alive
but hope is never lost
a flame of the undying kind

Trenches

you may think the storm has passed
but like storms often do
they take a break to let the sun shine through
before they once again flood you
it's why you should never wait
for the sun, to actually start living
but to learn how to dance in the pouring rain
so that storm won't overwhelm you
when it decides to come back again

rain dance

deep waters carry many secrets
and it takes a skilled diver
to bring them to the shore
out of this blue waved water
where secrets are no more
where they are laid bare in the sun
yet new secrets will form
where others come undone
for not all beauty should be known
life needs a little mystery
what would drive the diver to the ocean
if there was nothing new for him to see

beauty of the unknown

a change was coming
the turning of the wind
a magnetic shift
of unearthing proportion
storms brewing ahead
as lightning struck the water
waves growing and growing
crying out for a lifeline
until a whirlpool swallowed me whole
and I no longer knew
if there would ever be a moment
where my feet would touch the ground
but at the bottom of the ocean
sometimes clarity is found
and so it seems I learned to swim
as I emerged out of the water
taking a deep breath in
so I decided to float
and just give in to whatever it was
that taught me to swim
to just be for a while
and breathe it all in

the shift

she was born

a daughter

of spirit and earth

I am not fearless

as my ship navigates these waters

but because He believes in me

I know that fearless, is what I can be

II

THROUGH THE PRESENT

we either give up

or we keep rowing

towards the horizon

there is no in-between

you either give in to the water

and let your body drown

or you keep trusting in that spark

that keeps the air inside your lungs

that keeps you moving forward

that makes your ship sail on

no in-between

it is the journey that allows us to grow
it moulds us as life takes us forward
into whoever we need to be
in order to reach the destination
and even then
new journeys await

Transform

everything that you've been given
was always meant to grow beyond
something you could keep as your own
for can you say you've truly lived
when all you have, every gift
was always kept inside a box
as dust would settle right on top
and you never utilised, never even tried
to unwrap this hidden treasure
pieces that belong to you
for as you grow, they will too
every gift that you were given
has always been a light
to illuminate the world and other people's lives

given

there is no greater passion
that I have come to know
since music and its melodies
made my heart its home
through its pure melodic sound
images form inside my mind

where every note and every pause
take me on a journey, as sensation thaws
through sounds and visions unparalleled
making tears, in these eyes swell

of this beauty I'm allowed to see
as my words try to follow its melody
to describe this sense of sound
infusing every fibre, each and every bone
in that blissful moment I am truly home

when this art turns inside out
a fragility that is unbound
a passion play, a burning fire
ever stronger, ever brighter
that is what you do to me
this music is my poetry

artistic

SOMETIMES I FORGET

I CAN BE AS CRUEL AS THE SEA

WHEN I LET MY EMOTIONS

TAKE THE BEST OF ME

at times it's just too much
for my broken parts to handle
too many dreams at once, that I try to chase
wanting much yet doing nothing
too many things running around
inside my head

and I should just be quiet
let the tears run free
after all they only show
how it's overwhelming me

let the screams out of my lungs
let every breath I'm breathing in
bring me some tranquillity
sometimes it's a little too much
all of this fragility

fragile

He has more faith in us
than we have in ourselves
He knew of our successes
and failures to come
and still creation was carried on
created with the purest intention
a lingering wish
for us to reach our potential
knowing this world would blind many
and the ones who could see would be few
He still carries hope
for the souls which He made
He carries the greatest faith

His faith

faith does not come easy
it is a battle that is fought
between this world and the ego
that tries to keep us from the truth

and even then when trusting blindly
in the power of His word
there will be constant temptation
of an ego ridden world

and the more your faith will grow
the more you will be tested
as the strength of faith
is not build overnight

it's a path of trial and tribulation
one where you will reap what you sow
but when you stay the course
there will be a world of wonder
beyond anything you'll ever know

Through Trials

have you ever listened
to the rumbling mountains
and asked them why they roar
how it feels to be made up
from what's down in the earth's core
to be standing there for decades
imagine what they've seen
how it lets the trees embrace him
while the river flows
to well up from the mountaintop
and down below it goes
while to shake itself from its old fur
sometimes the mountain roars
and I wonder if that trembling's felt
deep within the earth's core
oh how mighty are these mountains
that we try to overcome
while they stand there quietly
basking in the sun
the perfect example of how it should be done
to take a moment and just be
one with nature
wild and free

mountains

our body and soul
are tethered by the finest
woven string
pure gold connecting them
from the moment we are born
that string starts to unravel
when we aren't taught to nurture it
and when we keep turning away

one day that string will snap
and you either come to realise
how important that string was
and you'll spend a lifetime trying
to weave that string back
or you'll turn away from trying
and never really care
that you become the ego
dark and unaware

...

...

that that fragile string
was so much more
than you could ever grasp
the lifeline to our life beyond
to beauty filled with wonders
to love infused with that pure gold
so much beyond what your heart can hold
but you will never know
the truth of who you are
of all that you can be
if you let it unravel like a cord
you will never see

string of gold

aren't we all travellers
in search of what feels like home
a place, a person, a feeling
wandering the earth
for a craving we all carry
home is what you've carried
all along, inside
so as far and as wide
as you may travel
wherever you may go
remember, that home is
what you already know

searchers

have you forgotten

completely

how to unfold

your wings

A TRAVELLING SOUL

he asked me
'would you not want to find
the path to immortality?'
I gently smiled and softly said
'I do not look for things that I already have'
from the baffled look upon his face
I knew he wasn't there yet
so this is what I then said

'as long as you look at immortality
as something made of flesh and blood
you will never understand
how you've misunderstood

all that you are and were meant to be
was never of this earth
as wonderful as this may seem
it was never meant to last
our chance for that, has long gone by
it is far in the past

you focus too much on the shell
though I know what's inside is hidden well
it's what's above and not below
that you should try to get to know
the source of our creation, the purest energy

...

...

yet somehow in His image, He created us to be
so maybe there's a point of truth
to what it is you think to know
but when He gave the breath of life
that's when you became alive

so you see it's not this flesh and blood
without this essence it would be no good
it is the soul, invisible to the eye
that is part of Him up high
that is where our resemblance lies

a part of immortality, that you are and always will be
so focus not on flesh and blood
but on that which you've not yet understood
it's when you quiet it all down
that in silence you will find
the voice of what you are

and when you let it merge, with this human mind
you will clearly see, maybe even a memory
of who and what and why
but you'll know that immortality
has always been within you and me'

search for immortality

there's time here
to self-reflect
to look at the things
that truly matter
there's time here
to connect
to whatever it is
that gives life meaning
to see what makes the sun rise
and set again at night
to look for what sparks joy
for the reasons you would fight
for every breath that holds a light
and makes every day
for you, worth while

breath of life

few things are more beautiful
than the stars that were created
a map spread out across the galaxies
nature has so much hidden mysteries
a book with stories to uncover
waiting there for someone to read
about its treasures, all its lessons
and all it takes is looking at the stars
to know where we are

star map

A TRAVELLING SOUL

you are the most beautiful example

of kindness and love

and how forgiveness knows no end

of being grateful for each and every day

to see beauty in simplicity

and find happiness

in the smallest of things

to speak without words

and trusting instinct

you are strong willed and determined

yet you also listen when asked right

it is for you that, whenever needed, I will fight

as all these lessons that you teach

are treasures we should keep

there are many things that we could learn

from the animals who walk this earth

for it is their love and trust which we must earn

paws

come hunt within the wilderness
the woodlands of my heart
come run along the trails and rivers
where sunlight rules and darkness quivers
where wolves are masters of the beat
the strong, wild pace that my heart keeps
spirits that are wild and free
wild horses running at the sea
vast waves of emotions
controlling ebb and flood
where instinct rules with life's intention
and nothing's ever misunderstood
for in this wild, compelling world all is as it seems
in this world there's only truth
no hidden mysteries

woodlands

paper hearts and salty seas
filled with oh so many tears
lessons learned, hard and true
some things they already knew
crumpled up, with hands they're torn
then paper cuts hands will adorn
a drop of blood, a ripple left
paper hearts, hurt and sad
through last defence, salty seas
send out their last tears
to imbue and then dissolve
broken hearts with tears convolve

paper hearts

no matter how much time's gone by
every tear that I still cry
hurts as much as it did then
in the deepest parts of me
will always lie a tragedy

agony

we tend not to believe
that which we cannot see
it was nothing different
with my disability

people only captured moments
but never saw the truth
the tears and pain that followed
after I smiled for you

it's a lesson that I learned
time and time again
that I should never hide
how I feel and who I am

show yourself

when you have little to no control

over how your body will react

and how your life will turn out

as a consequence of that

you try to find control in other things

and as small as they may be at first

they will surely grow

for as much as you try

you'll never succeed at filling that hole

we can only look at ourselves

and make changes where we can

even if our body isn't all

we wish that it would be

life is unpredictable

and it will always be

it was never meant to be controlled

by you or even me

control

YOUR FEAR OF LOSING PEOPLE

IS KEEPING YOU TRAPPED

INSIDE THE THOUGHT

YOU CAN'T MOVE ON FROM OTHERS

TO FOLLOW YOUR OWN PATH

as sad as every disaster is
sometimes the earth
needs to shake her skirt
to remind us
that we need to take better care
of her and each other
remember that the earth
has been through it all
waiting for us to see
and to finally stop
repeating history

disasters

written down, with every word
so many feelings left unheard
of how much unspoken things
have put a curse on this human being
darkness penetrates the mind
for words unspoken, are the kind
that are louder than words said
the ones that mess with the head
doubt and wonder do they sow
for the truth, it'll never know
but unspoken words, just like words said
are a mirror of he who hasn't spoken them yet
though they hurt the one who wished
that they would roll over their lips
they show what is or isn't there
revealing how much they truly care
in all that silence lies so much
almost tangible to the touch
yet not less painful, as you see
the truth in that mirror
sets unspoken words free

unspoken words

if He never gives us more
than we can handle
I wonder who I've been before
to make Him think
I am this strong

sometimes life
lets you hit a wall
so you can learn
how to climb it
through everything
we learn lessons
so we can overcome
what seemed impossible
and maybe that wall
always had a door
waiting for us to unlock it
maybe it is only build from the doubt
that lives inside you and me
and the moment we are past it
when we turn back to see
that wall has disappeared
because we finally believe

climb

your words have made many ripples
created many waves
they taught me how to sail my ship
to seek shelter in caves
that many look like diamonds
but are only made of glass
how it is best not to believe
to see through the mirage
of words that made up promises
that were never kept
each time, a ripple more
each time, a higher wave
until at one point I finally learned
how to navigate

Treacherous waters

from deep dark waters

I emerged a skilful diver

give it back to the waves
let it go with the pouring rain
so it does not last
but becomes ephemeral
and it doesn't weigh you down
longer than it has to
tears should never build an ocean
and yours built the dead sea
so give them back
for they do not belong
to be carried eternally

Tears

have I been rowing too long
in a boat that's making water
have I looked too much at the horizon
that I forgot to pay attention
to what's right before my feet

is there still time to mend
what I have broken
what I ripped apart in fear
of what it could be
papers floating on the water
words drowning in the sea

and I never told you
that I'm afraid to fly
how much it scares me to even try
even though these wings have always itched
I've been here for so long
trying to save a sinking ship

...

...

do you think there is still time
for me to make a change
to leave behind, these habits
these anchored fears of broken wings
these depths I've been diving in

I should leave it all behind
give it to the temper of the waves
unfold these wings, make a different choice
and fly towards what I've been staring at
the horizon never held the possibility
that was always right there before my feet
change has always been in me

not too late

95

and then He found me

a flower with a weakened stem

on the verge of breaking and He.

He made me whole again

let me sit here for a while
to take some time to ponder
about everything that's gone
and all that's still to come
about the memories I carry
and those that are yet to form
let me sit here for a while
to take some time to ponder
I will start on those
at dawn

a little time

because I looked at the beginning
I found you in the present
and walk beside you towards the future
fearless and bound by love
for all eternity to come

past, present, future

because of you I learned to love
and chase all that I am dreaming of
you are the wind that makes my voice take flight
my brightest star, my shining light
without you this world would not make sense
for every tear you wiped off my cheek
every cry for help you'd heed
you turned into a lesson learned
as I wonder how I've earned
a selfless love like yours
I hope I've given you a little
of all that you have given me
every moment with you, I've breathed in
now all that I can do
is shine a light for you
and for you, I will sing
for you gave my voice its wings

power of love

and it was as if I saw you
for the very first time
and the words you spoke
each one had a poetic line
and it awakened within me
what for a long time, was lost
and in that moment truth revealed
the man behind the mystery
and I, I love you even more
now that I know your history

visible

it's in those moments
where I know how you'd react
I hear your voice inside my head
and your void is overwhelming me
that little wonders are shown to me
where I am given opportunities

emanate

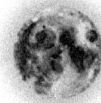

a light in the distance
guiding these weary bones
safely through this raging storm
every time that I feel lost
your light once again appears
so maybe now I look for those storms
to know that you're still near

lighthouse

do you ever fall asleep

to the rhythm of the beat

of the heart inside the chest

upon which you rest your head

soft whispers to your ear

a safe haven, conquering fear

for home is this right here

and your beat, it calms this heart

that's been a raging trap

but to the rhythm of your beat

I calm down and fall asleep

rhythmic

with you I long to count the stars
until we both are breathless
with you I'll wander near or far
whichever time or place
and I'll let every word you speak
imbue me in entirety
until no words are left to say
yet somehow they still find a way
as your eyes become what speak
oh, and in those counting moments
lest not forget that in my sleep
I'll count every caress
every kiss upon my cheek

countdown

can I give you my heart
as love overflows
will you keep it safe
as our love grows

can I share with you all
laughter and pain
will you learn how to dance
with me in the rain

can we sit here in silence
and hear beyond words
as we look at each other
can all be heard

through our bodies that speak
do you also feel, this love that I feel
then will you send me a letter
so I know that it's real

love letter

your eyes,

they sparkle like a million fireflies

your love,

so pure and innocent

your laughter,

like a bud unfolding

showing its beauty for the very first time

from your little hands, to your little feet

throughout all the firsts they'll come to meet

you are a wondrous creation

born from two hearts beating as one

and you,

my sweet, sweet child

deserve a salutation

new-born

HE CARRIES THE SUN

IN HIS EYES

AND I,

I AM COMPLETELY

AND IRREVOCABLY

MESMERISED

I can no longer let the fear of

living with a body that's a broken shell

keep me from exploring Your creation

after all You taught me well

there's nothing that I cannot accomplish

if my heart is true

and I keep walking in the direction

that brings me closer to You

walk by faith

how can I not love You more

when I carry within me

a part of Your soul

like a seedling sprouts

from the richest soil

I was drenched with Your light

and I carry Your glow

for in me is hidden

what eyes cannot see

the piece of Your soul

that You gave to me

forevermore

now more than ever
should we learn
to use our imagination
and become aware
of the power
that lies hidden
within the creativity
of our minds

now more than ever
should we learn
to set free
all that imagination
lets us see

world of imagination

it took me nearly a lifetime

to understand why my road

has been paved with sorrow

to see the beauty in all

that I have overcome

but most of all

to see the purpose of the roads

that I have taken

and the ones that lie ahead

it's clear now

who I was meant to become

the reasons behind everything

that was ever done

open eyes

and in the night.

He spoke to me..

His wisdom.

taking flight.

what is it

in this life

you seek

III

TOWARDS THE FUTURE

paint me a picture
of the world you'd like to see
of all the dreams you have
all you wish that you could be

paint me a picture
of the vision inside your head
of all the beauty
words have never said

paint me a picture
of untamed imagination
a world filled with sensation
paint in full coloration

painter

have you ever wondered
why the most important things in life
are invisible to the eyes
like the air we breathe
and the love we feel
and faith that keeps us on our feet
the most important things
aren't always meant to be seen
but to be felt in every fibre of our being
for the eyes may be the windows
but it's the soul that has all meaning
a wellspring waiting to be tapped
a silent hope patiently residing
until we can see without opening our eyes

invisible

dreams are like pebbles

skipping on the water

we cast them out into the world

but they do not always end up

becoming what we imagined

just like the pebbles skipping

from one place to another

dreams can change and they can grow

and like the ripples of the water

evolve into something

beyond what we thought to know

pebbles

everything that was
and everything that will be
somehow has always been
a thought, a fear, a dream
lingering beneath the surface
until it could be seen

underneath

SOMETIMES I WISH

IT HADN'T TAKEN ME A LIFETIME

TO FINALLY SEE

BUT PERHAPS

A LIFETIME WAS NEEDED

TO GROW INTO

WHO I'M MEANT TO BE

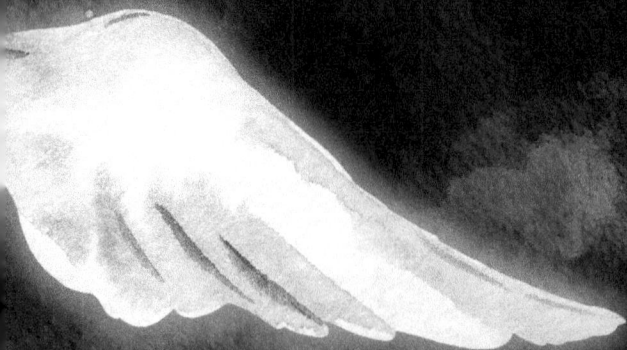

nothing He gave wasn't given intentionally
and everything that, upon my heart, was placed
the seeds He planted with His grace
were meant for me to grow
to make them bloom in their full glory
so even though life has sculpted me in many ways
this is only the beginning of my story

intentional

maybe we already knew
the consequences of the body
we would be in
and the life it would entail

maybe we accepted it fully
after seeing the bigger picture
after knowing the reasons why
even though all knowledge would be lost

never truly understanding
why we are born the way we are
until the day we die

lost knowledge

what you want may not be

what He wants for you

at the end of the road

when you ask Him:

'Lord, I've prayed for this so many times

and you never gave it to me.'

He will answer:

'My child, I gave you so many opportunities

but because it wasn't what you wanted,

you didn't see that it was what you needed.'

His Time

because He stands by patiently

watching me question everything

that I feel needs questioning

watching me explore every path

that I need to explore

knowing that

- in the end -

It will only bring me closer to Him

is why I love Him even more

freedom

the core of which
you were built
the ground stone
of your foundation
never alters
it is you who tries
to grow around it
in many different ways
some ways better than others
and more successful at some days
but the more you try to run from it
the heavier it's anchor will become
until you realise
it was foolish to run

fundamental

let me dance beneath the stars
let my heart run wild and free
along the river of life
on the journey You are taking me
where my soul is reunited
with the warm glow of its home
in nature's luminescence
let me freely roam

free

the shepherd leading his flock
never said the road would be easy
but that He would walk beside them
as they walk a difficult road
and lead them into safety

shepherd

my hunger for knowledge

grows...

like the waves of the sea

with every retraction

taking a little bit more with me

if you are afraid
of being confronted
with your true self
then what does that mean
that you are filled with darkness
too horrifying to see
or does it mean you're broken
and with it the light inside
and all that you could be

confrontation

what is it
that you want to leave
upon this earth
how do you wish
to be remembered

for every struggle shapes you
the best ones and the worst
but what truly matters
is how you've overcome
what troubles you the most

if you could look into the future
then what have you left behind
what do you want to be known for
your legacy to life

legacy

do you seek out to destroy
that which you do not understand
or do you try to expand your knowledge
so understanding may come to you

if the first, I can only hope
that you may one day see
that violence is not the answer
it will not cure stupidity

if the second, then I can only applaud
that you have come to realise
that you have so much more potential
and that knowledge can be grown
that you try to be understanding
to that which is different than your own

power of knowledge

LET IT GO

IT WEIGHS HEAVY

ON THE BEAUTY OF YOUR SOUL

LET IT GO

YOU WERE NEVER MEANT

TO CARRY AN EGO

giving in to judgement

to believe that bad things overrule

is easier than trying

to always see the good

to try and understand

there's more than meets the eye

in any given situation

and yet we still should try

for nothing was ever meant to be easy

the journey is how we grow

sometimes we need to work more

on letting things go

before we take a stand

form opinions and pass judgment

looking inwards before we look outside

for that is where love resides

judgement

it's always wise to think ahead
before words leave your mouth and are said
for every word creates a ripple
in the water that is life
that spreads out far beyond
yourself and your own mouth
so before you make a promise
you know you cannot keep
know that those make ripples
that run very deep

rippled water

from the very beginning we have fought

that, which we do not understand

and not once, has that ever brought forth

a better man

and right there
in that pit of your despair
I want to hold you
until you're ready to come up for air
and even then I will still hold you
so you know you're not alone
until you put one foot in front of the other
and you are standing on your own
then I'll still be there when you need me
for I too have known despair too long

not alone

the sea was restless as fresh air filled my lungs

I fell to my knees asking:

"Father, what is it that you want from me?"

but He knew I already had the answers

I could already see

far beyond what the world had shown me

for He made me an empath

absorbing it all

a smile could not hide

the anger and pain

nor could bitter words

hide a deep love and fear

so much was shown

overwhelming me

...

...

and so I sat there by the water

watching the waves swell and settle down

but if I am the waves

then You are my shore

always there calming me

bringing peace to my core

so I will stay the path

to share it with others

so the world that made them blind

may crumble before their eyes

and they may know, that no matter what

You are and have always been

waiting at the shoreline

for the waves to come rolling in

waiting

when you've run out of faith
I will be here waiting
for I carry enough for both of us
and when you are ready
and your soul is replenished
you'll know where I'll be
right there where you lost it
and where you left me

undying faith

WE ARE ALL CAPABLE

OF DARKNESS

BUT EVERY TIME

WE CHOOSE NOT TO

WE FEED THE LIGHT

WITHIN US

AND WITH THAT

IT GROWS STRONGER

THAN DARKNESS COULD EVER BE

change is inevitable

no matter how much you try

to fight it...

..... in the end

you must evolve

it flew by as though it never existed
and yet so much had changed
tangible yet untouchable
like melting ice stinging feeble hands
leaving a mark upon the skin
forever changed deep within

Time

I will not say that it gets better
that after a while the hurt subsides
as molecules are forever changed
once you start to grow around the pain
and every single day
there is no other choice but to move forward
as you learn to breathe again
and the branches of your sorrow
entangle the hole inside your chest
and as you take life day by day
you will come to understand
the worthiness of love and effort
and simply letting go
for loss has many lessons
that you will come to know

Through loss

if love can go on
long after someone's gone
then why could life itself
not be infinite
as love is born out of life
and life born out of love
then why would you think
that life is not eternal
that it could not go on
just like love
long after someone's gone

infinite

don't wait for it to find you
but look for it yourself
don't think that you're unworthy of it
this emptiness is not forever
this void can be made whole
you are far too precious to believe
that love and happiness is found in things
true love and happiness always start within
a dormant spark you can awaken
if you choose to believe
that through consciously living
there is much you can achieve

deserving

WHO'S TO SAY

THAT WHERE YOU ARE

IS NOT EXACTLY

WHERE YOU ARE NEEDED

sand and stone beneath my feet
as I leave my ship to come ashore
another world, should I explore?
is there time to learn something more
for this heart, with wanderlust is filled
and this need for knowledge is unstilled
but now here do I stand alone
where two were meant to build a home
yet if not now, then who knows when
for who knows what is hidden on this land
if I do not take a leap of faith
who knows what wonders will come my way
to explore, I must, is what you'd say
so here I go and tread this land
to plant some roots in stone and sand

explorer

may you find a little peace
amidst of all the chaos
may you spend a little time
to nurture your own light
may blessings befall upon you
through all your darkest times
may love forever fill you
even when you don't feel loved
may your eyes be opened wide
to everything that feeds your light
may your courage be forever strong
as you carve out your life, your home

blessing

in the end

we are what we believe

we are worthy of being

which is either good or bad

but believing in yourself

is the strongest form of magic

you will ever have

if there's anything
you'd like to ask Him
then ask that your eyes may be opened
to all that He has given you
but for which you were too blind to see

ask

sometimes I just stand there
watching as the world goes by
changing, evolving
and I just stand there watching
and wondering about the why
and how of things
as life passes by

because sometimes it's overwhelming
when you come to realise
how small we are in all of this
like little leaves on the tree
that carries the universe on its branches
a tiny speck in the galaxy

those are the things
that I carry within me
how we walk on a small piece
of something so magnificent
so I just stand here watching
wondering where it all will end

magnificence

there is no ending to this life

but yes, this world is fleeting

it's only when we shine
His light upon this world
that there is still hope of saving
everything He once envisioned
and wished for us to have

future

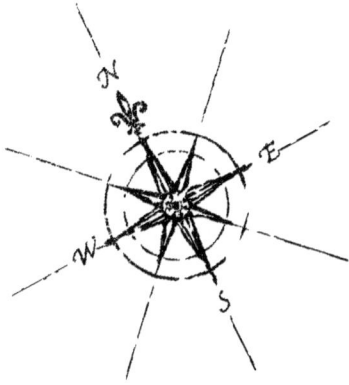

to the North,
where the stars shine bright
and my eyes, they are mesmerized
to the East,
where dreams awaken
with the rising of the sun
to the South,
where my heart is set on fire
and love is flowing free
to the West,
where the magic of the day
turns into wonders of the night
come away with me
and follow the compass of life

compass

a heart is not some fragile thing
it's the backbone that makes you sing
every time it's touched by love
gentle and soft melodies
prepare it for a symphony
a love intense and firm
that awakens all your senses
that teaches you all there is to learn
know that the time will come
when you will burst out into song

love song

I have searched for you
for what feels like a thousand years
my heart awakened by your light
all this love that lives inside of me
this passion I no longer have to hide
for with you all the pieces fall into place
and forever no longer feels
like a loneliness I have to face

awakened

my love, could I ask of you

to love me in wholes, not in halves

with all my imperfections

to listen to understand, not to give an answer

to be faithful at all times

try not to break my heart

it beats strongest by your side

to never tell me lies

no matter how hard the truth

to never make a promise

that you don't intend to keep

as you know those things

would hurt deeply and make me weep

to communicate your feelings and intentions

even when you don't feel like it at times

know that you can tell me

whatever is on your mind

...

...

to acknowledge my emotions
no matter how they come
to share my laughter
yet not shy away from tears
to accept my health with all its flaws
the good days and the bad
without feeling you should save me
but to stand by me as I save myself
even when times get hard
to love me even then
to look beyond my disabilities
for they do not define who I am

could I ask this of you
if so then I am truly blessed
to have you by my side
what I ask of you, I give without hesitation
my love I say 'I do'
to this journey of a lifetime with you

vows

LOVE RESIDES

IN MANY THINGS

BUT IN THE SMALLEST GESTURE

ITS TRUEST FORM

IS OFTEN FOUND

I'm not afraid of dying

for it means I'm going Home

I'm afraid of not having done enough

with everything He gave me

that I have not shown enough

of His glory to the world

I'm more afraid of disappointing Him

with all the gifts He gave me

dying is not one of them

for my soul has always known

that this is not its home

endings

I hope the sails on your ship

catch a steady wind

and the water stays a calm force

cradling your ship with a steady pace

I hope that the sun will shine upon you

now your journey has begun

that you capture many moments

as you sail towards the setting sun

setting sail

come sit with me in silence
just for a little while
do you see now that there's still hope
and light still shines in this world
have I shown you enough
have these words touched you in any way
to carry the light within yourself
out into the world
do you see how you are the hope
of the future
how you never have and never will
walk this earth alone
that you are loved beyond measure
and are more than enough
for what is within you
is made of love and stardust

enough

my love is like an ocean

deep and evergrowing

I hope one day, a love like that...

..you may come to know it

it is a journey with no end

for love does life itself transcend

THE END IS ONLY

THE BEGINNING

OF AN UNDISCOVERED

JOURNEY

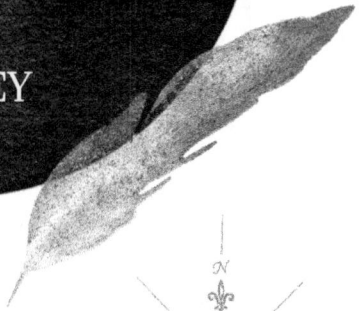

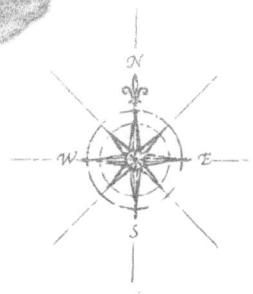

WITH LOVE,

Lizzy

www.ingramcontent.com/pod-product-compliance
Lightning Source LLC
LaVergne TN
LVHW052026080426
835513LV00018B/2188